Mortgage Loan Secrets

How to Get a Mortgage in less than 30 days

Table of Contents

Chapter One: Mortgage basics 3

Chapter Two: The Loan Process 11

Chapter Three: Loan Types 19

Chapter Four: Interest Rates...33

Chapter Five: Where do you get a loan?.......................................37

Chapter Six: The Actual Mortgage 39

Introduction

Most buyers are unfamiliar with the process of getting a loan and what it really takes to get approved. They get frustrated with all the paperwork and they feel like they are asked for the same items over and over and over again. Most buyers don't really know what buying power they have. I see both ends of the scale: people who feel they can afford twice as much as allowed, and others who could qualify for five times more than they want. Also, there are various loan programs, down payment options, and the types of lenders who are available. All these options can make your head spin.

The industry is constantly changing, which can confuse a buyer. The questions I hear most often are: "What is the interest rate?" and "What is my payment?" Although both are very valuable questions, they are not necessarily the critical ones when it comes to getting a mortgage.

Finding the ideal loan officer is crucial and critical in getting you through the preapproval stage and all the way to the closing table. As an experienced business owner and loan officer, I have read the thousands of pages of regulations, and studied the various loan programs, in order to help my buyers get into the right program, at the right time, and for the right reasons.

When purchasing real estate, and using a home loan or mortgage, there are so many variables to be considered. Do I get an FHA, VA, RD or a conventional loan, or do I get what is called a non-qualified mortgage? Do I need to worry about PMI — and what exactly is that? Do I get a variable rate or a fixed rate? Does the length of time I plan on living in the house matter? Each state and local entity has some of their own costs and rules. After reading this book, you will have an understanding of what is needed, why you should work with a qualified and experienced loan officer, and be ready to breeze through the process.

My mantra is education, communication, and certainly having some fun along the way. Life is too short, so, you better enjoy what you are doing. Because of this, I have put together a helpful guide and reference material to assist you, the buyer, in understanding the process and to help you through that process seamlessly so you aren't pulling out your hair.

Chapter One

Mortgage basics

Just as homes come in various styles and different price ranges, so, too, are the ways you can finance them. There are many types of loans and many options from which to choose. If you, as a buyer, understand this and do some work in advance, you will have fewer challenges throughout the process.

Mortgage lenders have to review an application, and all the supporting documents, very carefully in order to be confident that you will repay your loan. I often hear, "Well, I didn't need all that information, and I just got a loan to buy a car." That may be true; however, it is also a lot easier to repossess a car than a home. Lenders like to lend money and have you pay them back. They are not interested in owning house if you default. So, in deciding whether you are "worthy" of a loan, you will often hear about the four C's in getting a loan: credit, capacity, collateral, and capital. Let's take a look at why these are important to a lender.

Credit

The lender pulls a credit report from all three repositories; TransUnion, Equifax, and Experian. While it may surprise some, each consumer has multiple credit scores. There are several reasons why. First, most consumers have credit information at each of the three major credit bureaus. While the credit data should generally be the same from one credit bureau to the next, there are often minor differences. These differences can result in three different credit scores, even if the score is generated by the same credit scoring model. Each of your items, like a credit card, or an installment loan, is called a trade line—and not all tradelines report to all bureaus.

There are also different credit scoring models. Even within the main FICO (Fair Isaac Corporation) systems, the scores will vary depending on the type of loan you are getting. I often hear, "That can't be my score. I just bought a car and my score was totally different." Yes, each type of lender can use a different FICO Score version. Auto lenders, for instance, often use FICO® Auto Scores, an industry-specific FICO Score version that's been tailored to their needs. Most credit card issuers, on the other hand, use FICO® Bankcard Scores or FICO® Score 8. Other vendors may use the Vantage scoring system.

It turns out that the most widely used FICO score for mortgage lenders is the FICO Score 8. That's true even though FICO Score 9 has been released. Although your credit score may not be the same as on the one you pull on creditkarma.com, for example, it should trend in the same direction. I have often instructed my buyers to pull their own scores at creditkarma.com, or another source, and monitor it if they aren't ready to have a lender pull their credit and track it on a weekly basis.

So, what is a good credit score? In each of the loan programs, I will discuss the credit scores that are acceptable. FICO scores run from 300 to 850. The numbers are important to lenders because there is a strong correlation between scores and future delinquency. Listed below are the ranges and the likelihood of delinquency in the future.

Exceptional—800 and above: Only 1% are likely to become seriously delinquent in the future.

Very Good—740 to 799: Only 2% are likely to become seriously delinquent in the future.

Good—670 to 730: Approximately 8% are likely to become seriously delinquent in the future.

Fair—580 to 669: Approximately 28% are likely to become seriously delinquent in the future.

Poor—579 and lower: Approximately 61% are likely to become seriously delinquent in the future.

No one knows the exact algorithm for determining your score (except those that write it, of course). However, after looking at thousands of credit reports, we have a good idea of what plays into the score.

As far as what makes up credit scores, it's the following:

Mortgage basics

1. Payment history (the longer the better): 35%. If you have a history of paying your bills on time all the time, you can positively affect your credit score. Late or missed payments will negatively affect your credit score.

2. Debt to credit ratio, or the amount you owe on credit and debt, (the lower the better): 30% . This is the total amount of credit you actually are using (balances), compared to the total amount you have available, and this is your utilization. The lower the number, the better, and a ratio below 30% is ideal. For example, if your limit on a card is $1,000 and you owe $950, you have a 95% utilization; whereas, if your balance is $250, you have a 25% utilization. Even if you pay all your bills on time (which is excellent), when your balances are near their limits, lenders get nervous, as your ability to pay seems to decrease if there is a sudden drop in income.

3. Time in bureau (the longer the better): 15%. Because past behavior is a good indication of future behavior, the scoring models look back and consider how long you have used credit, including oldest and newest accounts. In general, it is better to have a longer credit history than a shorter one.

4. Types of credit (mix of credit cards & installment loans): 10%. The types of credit are also a factor. Scoring models look at how many credit cards and installment loans there are, and if the credit cards are the same type. For example, do you have all retail cards, or all revolving accounts.

5. New credit (new accounts and inquiries): 10%. Finally, a lender looks at how many times you request credit that generates a hard inquiry. Too many hard inquiries will negatively affect your credit. A lot of people around the holidays tend to open new cards because they get a "deal or a discount" on their purchases. If you are in the process, or soon to be in the process of purchasing a new home, this is not the time to open new credit cards. Now, once your loan officer pulls your credit, they may very well suggest that you open a new card to build your credit. This is a strategy that should be discussed with your loan officer.

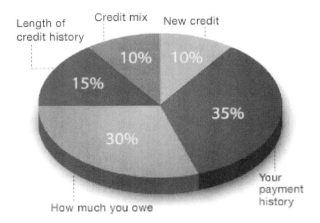

You may be asking yourself, what if I am just shopping around for a loan and now I have different lenders pulling my credit. How bad will that hurt my score? First, there is a difference between a soft pull and a hard pull. A soft pull happens without you even knowing it and it does not affect your credit score. Sometimes, these can happen when you aren't even aware it is happening. For example, when you receive that unsolicited credit card offer in the mail, or when a perspective employer does a background check. The other popular one is when you pull the credit report yourself, or you are working with a certified finance agency, whose goal is get you "credit ready" to purchase. None of these will affect your credit score.

A "hard pull" can affect your score. When shopping for a loan it is common to contact different financial institutions and speak with multiple lenders. A lender will pull your credit to determine your scores and these are hard pulls. The time lag between rate shopping, so it only counts as one pull, varies within a fourteen to forty-five-day window. The credit bureaus realize you are shopping around and not getting multiple mortgages. The pulls can stay on your credit report for two years; however, it will only affect your score for one year. So, if you are shopping around, you want to do it within the grace period of one pull.

Mortgage basics

Capital

Capital refers to the financial resources that a borrower may have in order to deal with their current debt and their future "new home loan" debt. Borrowers who have a down payment to put on a home, generally find it easier to get a mortgage. Even programs (discussed later) that require little to no down payment often will require at least one to three months of house payments saved or available in case of emergency. The less "financially invested" in a property, the more likely the buyer will just "walk away" if things go bad. Lenders do not like defaulted loans—it affects their ability to lend in the future on specific programs.

Capacity

Capacity measures a buyer's ability to repay a loan. The lender compares current income against recurring debts, and analyzes what is called the borrower's DTI, or debt to income. The DTI is calculated by adding together all the current recurring debt and the new house payment (including taxes, insurance, home owner association fees, and principal and interest) and dividing it by the gross monthly income. The lower the DTI, the better the chance of qualifying for a loan. All lenders are different, but often follow the agencies' guidelines, and traditionally like to keep the DTI below 41-45%. Recurring debt includes minimum monthly credit card payments, installment loans (cars, RV's), alimony, student loans (even if in deferment), child support, personal loans, and other home loans you may continue to keep (like an investment property or second home).

Example:

	Annual	Monthly
Buyer #1 income	$48,000	$4,000
Buyer #2 income	$36,000	$3,000
Total Income		$7,000
Current Monthly debt		
Student loan	$50,000	$500
CC min payment		$80
CC min payment		$25
Car		$280
New House payment		$2,000
Total debt		$2,885
DTI		41.21%

Collateral

Collateral is the value of the property that the buyer is purchasing. This is determined by the appraisal that the lender will order. The lender needs to verify that the price you are paying for a home is in fact "worth" that amount. Most realtors price the house they are selling within the proper price range, as they would have done what is called a comparable analysis. Therefore, if you offer "above" the asking price, you stand the chance it may not appraise and, in some contracts, the seller expects you to bring that difference to the closing table. In other cases, the deal can just be withdrawn, or negotiated or, if there is evidence with other recent sales, the realtor may be able to provide additional documentation to the appraiser justifying the price. It is best for your realtor to provide this information to the appraiser prior to their analysis, as some lenders will not allow you to contest the amount.

Mortgage basics

<u>Character</u> – A Bonus C

The lender will also look at whether the buyer has had a foreclosure or bankruptcy in the past and how long ago. Each loan program has its own guidelines. In addition, the lender will look at employment history, whether the buyer has a steady job, and the type of income.

Chapter Two

The Loan Process

Okay, now that you have decided you have pretty good credit, saved a little bit of money, paid your bills on time, and you have a steady job, what do you do next, and what are the steps to getting that elusive loan?

The first step is to contact your loan officer and get preapproved, not just prequalified.

Preapproved vs Prequalified

Many people think of both preapproved and prequalified as the same thing. Unfortunately, those qualifiers are not the same. You want to make sure you are preapproved. Prequalified simply means your loan officer pulled credit and asked you some questions. Based on your answers and your credit report, they determine whether you are prequalified, and they send you on your happy way to look at houses with your realtor. There have been many times when a realtor has called me to "save the day" because someone was prequalified but, when the file was "turned in" and reviewed by an underwriter, the buyer is denied. Why does this happen? Because all the documents weren't reviewed in advance by the loan officer. This is an excellent reason to work with an experienced loan officer.

When a loan officer preapproves a person, that means they reviewed all the necessary documents and reviewed the credit report very carefully. So, what are those documents?

What Documents Will my Loan Officer Need?

Income documents

It is the lender's responsibility to evaluate income stability, adequacy, and likelihood of continuance. So, the first step is to determine what type of income the borrower is receiving: salary, hourly, commission, piecework, self-employed, disability, non-taxable, or retirement.

Generally speaking, if you are receiving any kind of variable income, like commission, overtime, part-time, piecework, or are self-employed, it is considered stable and useable if you have been receiving it for two years. It also needs to be steady or increasing to consider it as stable. Traditionally, lenders average this type of income. However, if the income has declined over the past two years, we cannot average and, in many cases, may not be able to use this type of income. Your lender will ask for at least thirty days of paycheck stubs, in addition to the previous two years' W2s or tax returns (especially if self-employed), to verify this income.

If you are self-employed, you will usually file a Schedule C or have corporation documents. You will need to provide all the pages of your Federal tax return. Your lender will do an analysis of your returns to determine what income can actually be used for qualifying. There are certain items, like business miles or business use of your home, that may be added back to your net income. Usually, you need to be in business for at least two tax years to use the income, as self- employed income is variable and, therefore, no guarantee of continuance. Your lender will usually average the income from the previous two years. In addition, if you have had more than a 20% decline in the last years of your income, a lender may not be able to use it. There are some programs that allow you to use the latest one year of income for self-employment, as long as you have been in business for at least five years, and have the ability to prove it, for example, an original license.

Newly acquired retirement, disability, or some other forms of nontaxable income, do not have to have a two year history provided they have a guarantee of a minimum three year continuance.

I often get asked the question, "Do I have to be on the same job for two years?" The answer is not necessarily. If you are moving to another full-time position, at either a salary or an hourly rate, as long as we can verify it, and we can receive thirty days of documentation, you should be good. Remember though, we also look at employment history. Are you switching jobs frequently, or are you moving because of advancements, or utilizing your education? Valid reasons for job changes are acceptable. We also make sure there are not job gaps over the previous two years.

The good news is, if you have been a full-time student and are now employed and wanting to purchase a home, you do not have to be on your job for two years, as normally we can count schooling as employment with proper documentation.

Asset documents

It is the lender's responsibility to verify the asset documents and to review them and make sure all is copacetic. We will look at the latest two months of all asset documents. We look for any deposits that are not payroll deposits. All large deposits must have full documentation on the source of the deposit. Each loan program will define a large deposit slightly differently. It is best to speak with a loan officer before depositing non-payroll money.

For example, with a conventional loan, for any single non-employment deposit that is less than 50% of the qualified monthly income, we do not need additional documentation. However, for other types of loans, we may need documentation. We will also look to see if there are insufficient fund charges. We do understand that mistakes can happen and, as long as we have a valid explanation, you should be fine. However, if you have multiple and recurring charges, this can indicate the inability to manage your money and is of concern to a lender.

We will also look at any other person that is on the bank statement but not on the loan. Because we will be using these funds, the "non-borrowing" co-owner of the account will have to sign a letter stating they realize the funds are being used for the loan.

Gift money is also something that we have to monitor very closely. Each loan program handles gift money slightly differently. Essentially we have to verify the source of all gift funds and they must come from a "qualified" donor, usually a family member but not always. In addition, on many programs we will need a copy of the donor's bank statement showing they in fact had the funds available to gift. They will also sign a document stating that funds are truly a gift and are not required to be repaid. Before you deposit any gift money in your bank account, speak with your loan officer to follow the proper procedures.

Depending on the rest of your profile, gift money can be looked on negatively by the lender. If you do not have any of your own funds saved, and all the money is gifted, the lender will look at other items more closely, like credit score, other obligations, and debt to income, etc. One of the biggest defaults on a home loan is when the majority of the funds are gifted and the buyer has no other resources to pay their monthly bills when an emergency arises.

Retirement documents are usually only needed when we are using the funds for either the loan or if a reserve is required. If retirement funds are needed, and the borrower is not of retirement age, the lender will also need the documentation that states the "terms and conditions" for which the money can be withdrawn. All programs are slightly different. The good news is, if you have to borrow money from your retirement plan, and you then are put on a payment plan to repay it, we do not have to count the debt in your overall debt to income, because it is your own money.

Other documents

Often a lender will require the latest two years of tax returns, even if you are not self-employed. The reason for this is that we have to verify there is nothing else in the return that would raise a flag, like a part-time business that you are taking as a loss or a rental income loss.

If you have been divorced in the last seven years, a lender may need a copy of your divorce decree. The lender has to make sure there are no obligations that you are required to pay, like spousal or child support, a portion of the sale of a property, or paying off debt, etc.

Do you have a child support document? If so, the lender will need that, too. If your divorce decree states your spouse is required to pay, and you are not using the income, then you won't need the document (on most loans). However, if you are receiving child support and wish to use it for qualification, the lender will need to see that you have received it consistently to be able to count it. For some loans, you will need to show receipt for three months and, for others, six months. You will also have to demonstrate that it will continue for at least three years from the date of the close of your loan.

Do you have a rental or investment property or second home or land? If so, you will need documentation showing your mortgage payment, taxes, insurance, and any homeowners association dues. If you have had an investment property for the previous tax year, you will probably have a Schedule E with your taxes. If you do, that can often be provided instead of the listed documents and your lender will compute whether it can be counted as income or loss. However, what you report over the last two years on your tax returns will be what is used.

If you are a veteran and using a VA loan, you will need a copy of your certificate of eligibility, or at least your DD-214, so your lender can order the certificate of eligibility.

Part of the home loan process is to make sure you, as a buyer, meet the debt to income guidelines, have sufficient assets, and a good history of paying your bills. Lenders follow all the agency guidelines when doing a qualified loan. The last thing a lender wants is to have a loan in default because they didn't do their due diligence up front. This can hurt a lender's ability to continue to finance future loans.

Your lender will continue to monitor all your finances during the loan process. Even throughout the process, they may ask to update certain documents as documents can only be so old when the loan is closed. The lender may even verify your employment the day of close to make sure you are still employed. If you are planning on making any job changes, or major financial purchases that will either affect your current balances or require you to open new credit, you need to notify your loan officer immediately because this can affect your ability to get a loan. Sometimes buyers think they are helping by opening another credit card with lower interest rates and transferring their balances. The lender will be notified when any new credit is pulled and it will require you as a buyer to produce more documentation to verify you are not taking on any additional debt. Below are general suggestions for you.

Dos and don'ts when buying a house

Do's

- ➤ Continue to make your rent or mortgage payments on time.
- ➤ Stay current on all other existing accounts.
- ➤ Continue to use your credit as normal.
- ➤ Be prepared to explain any large deposits.
- ➤ Do continue to work your normal work schedule with no unplanned time off.
- ➤ Keep financial records close at hand.

Do NOTS

- ➤ Do NOT make any major purchase.
- ➤ Do NOT apply for ANY new credit (even if you are preapproved or same as cash) or open any new credit.
- ➤ Do NOT close any credit cards (without lender approval).
- ➤ Do NOT pay off charges or collections (unless your Loan Officer directed you to).
- ➤ Do NOT consolidate your debts.
- ➤ Do NOT make unusual deposits or open new bank accounts.
- ➤ Do NOT change banks.
- ➤ Do NOT have any insufficient fund charges.
- ➤ Do NOT spend money you saved for down payment.
- ➤ Do NOT deposit gift money until you speak to me about the process.
- ➤ Do NOT change jobs, change your pay type, or reduce your hours.
- ➤ Do NOT cosign for anyone.
- ➤ We look at everything for the previous two months and throughout the loan process. Make this the most boring time of your life with your finances.

The Closing

There are three buckets of money that a buyer needs to bring to the closing. The first is the down payment and this is determined by the loan product. The second bucket is the reserves and prepaids.

The Loan Process

These include interest charges from the day you close until the end of the month, one year's homeowners insurance, and an escrow for property tax and home insurance to pay the future bills. The third bucket is the closing costs. Pretty much anyone who touches your loan gets a fee. For example, appraiser, origination or underwriting, title or escrow agent, recording fees, or credit reports and monitoring are some of the fees.

It is important for the loan officer to select the proper program so you have enough funds for each of the buckets. In addition, most loan programs require you to have additional money, called reserves, to cover at least one to three months of future house payments. The lender needs reassurance that, if an emergency comes up, you still have the ability to make your payments.

Chapter Three

Loan Types

The loan officer helps to decide the correct loan program. Loans come in many sizes and flavors. There are four basic types of loans and hundreds of variations. Now, the question becomes, what type of loan should you get? This is where your loan officer earns his or her money. They need to be familiar with all the loan types and calculate what is best for you.

Conventional

Many people still think that you need 20% down for a conventional loan. That is not true. Depending on your income, you can go as low as 3% and, even if you do not meet the 3% down program, 5% is the minimum required. However, if you put less than 20% down, you will be required to carry Private Mortgage Insurance or PMI. PMI is a layer of protection for the lender. It is also an added expense to the borrower. However, it does allow you to get into a home with less than 20% down. This is a protection for the lender in case you end up in foreclosure. This does not protect you if you fall behind in your payments. The cost of PMI will vary depending on how much you are putting down and your credit scores.

So, this insurance is typically paid monthly and, when your equity based on payments reaches 78% of your purchase price, the PMI payments should end. If you make no extra payments, this is roughly seven years. So, let's say your house appreciates and now your house is worth more, can you cancel your PMI? Maybe. You could refinance and, if the value came in, then, yes, your new loan would not have PMI. However, if you don't want to refinance, you just want to cancel PMI, you have to jump through some hoops because it isn't automatic. You could be required to pay for an appraisal that the lender or servicer will order. You usually have to request the cancellation in writing. You have to be current on all your payments. You might have to prove you do not have any other liens on the house. Also, you might have had to make at least twenty-four monthly payments. Before you pay for the appraiser, contact your

Mortgage Loan Secrets

lender or servicer and find out their requirements for removing PMI before the normal time frame.

To add to your confusion, PMI can be paid monthly (which is most of the time), up front, or a combination. This is where your loan officer needs to discuss those options with you. Usually, if you pay upfront, you do not get any refund if your value goes up. This does mean that you will not have that fee every month, and it will lower your debt to income, potentially qualifying you for a larger home.

The minimum qualifying credit score for a conventional loan is currently 620.

Loans can be used for primary, secondary, or investment properties that are one to four units. Anything above four units is considered a commercial property and must get a commercial (nonresidential) loan.

A buyer can ask the seller to pay for closing costs and prepaids, however, the amount they can ask for is limited to how much of a down payment they putting down. It can vary between 3% to 9% of the sales price for a primary home and 2% for an investment property.

Borrowers must wait to apply for a conventional loan for four years after bankruptcy 7 discharge, or two years with an acceptable extenuating circumstance. After a Chapter 13, it is four years from discharge date or two years from dismissal date. You must also re-establish a positive credit history during that period.

For a conventional loan, you must wait seven years from date of foreclosure, or three years from foreclosure with acceptable extenuating circumstances, and an additional down payment is required. For a short sale, deed in lieu, or mortgage charge off, it is four years from the date the sale closed and transferred to a new owner or two years with extenuating circumstances.

For a conventional loan, an extenuating circumstance is a nonrecurring event beyond the borrower's control that resulted in a sudden, significant, and prolonged reduction in income, or a catastrophic increase in financial obligations. It must be verified and documented. Divorce is not considered extenuating.

Loan Types

Federal Housing Administration (FHA)

An FHA loan is a government backed mortgage insured by the Federal Housing Administration or FHA. The FHA is an arm of the Department of Housing and Urban Development (HUD). The minimum down payment is 3.5%. FHA loans also have a version of PMI called MIP or Monthly Insurance Premium, which is based simply on the down payment amount, not the credit score, making it occasionally less expensive for lower credit than a conventional loan. Unlike conventional loans, this fee does not go away when you have certain equity in the property, when only putting the minimum 3.5% down. It remains for the life of the loan. So, the only way to remove the MIP is to refinance into a conventional loan, or sell the house and close the loan, or pay off the loan.

In addition, FHA charges an up-front funding fee, currently at 1.75% of the loan amount, which just gets added to your base loan. This fee is what finances the FHA program for defaulted loans.

FHA technically allows a borrower to have as low as a 500 credit score with 10% down. However, many lenders will not offer this program as it is too risky. The lowest credit score a lender will allow is typically between 580 and 620 and each lender's risk tolerance is slightly different. In these cases, your minimum down payment is 3.5%.

On this type of loan, you can ask the seller to pay up to 6% of qualified closing costs and prepaids. This can limit your out-of-pocket expenses and allows more buyers to purchase a home. In many cases, your realtor will expect you to increase the amount you offer to the seller by the amount you are asking in concessions. So, for example, if you are purchasing a $100,000 home, and requesting the seller to pay 6% toward closing costs and prepaids ($6,000), your realtor may suggest you offer $106,000 so your bid stays competitive with someone offering $100,000 and no concessions. The concessions come off the amount the seller receives at close, so, if you did not increase your price, essentially the seller is only receiving $94,000 instead of the asking price of $100,000. I am removing all normal costs the seller pays in this example to compare apples to apples.

Even though the purchase price for you has gone up, the difference in the monthly payment is usually well worth the savings in cash.

FHA loans are only used for primary homes and you typically can only have one FHA loan at a time. There are a couple of conditions where a second is allowed, for example, when you have a primary home with an FHA loan and you are transferred more than 100 miles away for work and need to purchase another home. If you don't sell your current home first, you must qualify for both payments along with all your other debt.

The property must be appraised by an FHA-approved appraiser and meet HUD (Housing and Urban Development) property guidelines. Often, when you do your initial inspection on the house, your inspector will be familiar with the HUD guidelines and can give you an idea whether the appraiser will call for any repairs. Traditionally, if a house is listed with FHA financing, then the seller has already agreed to correct any repairs the appraiser has indicated. Once the repairs are complete, the appraiser will have to go back out and do a reinspection before the loan can close. The reinspect fee is paid by the buyer and usually disclosed up front. Occasionally, if a repair cannot be done due to weather, the lender will hold in escrow approximately one and a half times the highest bid until the work is complete. The money that is held back provides some security for the lender and the buyer, if for some reason the work is not completed as promised, and the lender can find someone else to do the work and has the funds to do it. Many lenders will require one to three bids and will take the highest bid for escrow purposes. After the lender is satisfied the work has been completed, they will pay the vendor who did the work and reimburse the difference to the party that had the funds withheld. In addition, usually the buyer has to pay a fee for this service and will be notified, and it will be included on the closing statement. Escrow holdbacks are risky, so, not all lenders will allow escrows and most will only allow due to weather issues, for example, painting that is required on an outside building but the weather will not allow the work to be done.

Borrowers must wait to apply for an FHA loan for two years after bankruptcy and three years after a foreclosure. They must also

Loan Types

re-establish a positive credit history during that period. There are occasions where the time frame can be shortened, if there were extenuating circumstances, like a serious illness or death of a wage earner. Divorce or inability to sell a property due to a job transfer or relocation is not considered extenuating.

Rural Development (RD) or USDA

If you are thinking of buying a house in the "country" and you meet other requirements, this might be the program for you. This is a 0% down loan guaranteed by the USDA (United States Department of Agriculture and Rural Development). You will still need money for closing costs and prepaids, however, you can ask the seller to pay up to 6% of the sales price toward those costs. So, theoretically, you can get into a new home, for very little to no money. This program helps lenders and is designed to provide affordable homeownership opportunities for low to moderate income families living in rural areas.

This program is also designed for a primary home. The buyer cannot own a primary residence at the time they close the new loan.

There are some other restrictions, like household income cannot exceed a certain amount, and this is based on your location in the country. Check with your local lender to see what the limit is in your area. Even though everyone in the household may not be on the loan, the lender must count all income toward the limits. The exception to the rule is, if you are a full-time student over the age of 18, and not the spouse of the buyer, a lender does not have to count their earnings.

In addition, there are some asset limitations. If the buyer has enough non-retirement funds to purchase the home with 20% down, they will not qualify.

To check and see if the home you are interested in qualifies go to:

https://eligibility.sc.egov.usda.gov/eligibility/welcomeAction. do?pageAction=sfp

RD loans also have a monthly funding fee of .35% of the loan amount and an up-front fee of 1% that is added to the loan amount.

Mortgage Loan Secrets

These fees are much lower than FHA fees and often lower than conventional fees.

The minimum credit score for a buyer is 620; however, realistically, depending on the buyer's reserves and other items, it will usually require a higher score. RD has their own modeling system that lenders must run through a program to see if all the criteria fit. For example, does the buyer have reserves (remember, it is possible with full concessions and 0% down, the buyer could essentially bring no money to close), or have they had a history of making on-time rent or house payments. Your lender will run some scenarios through the automated system before issuing a preapproval.

Borrowers must wait to apply for an RD loan for three years after bankruptcy and three years after a foreclosure. They also have to re-establish a positive credit history during that period. There are occasions where the time frame can be shortened if there were extenuating circumstances. Loss of job, delay or reduction in government benefits or other loss of income, increased expenses due to illness or death, will be considered. Circumstances must be out of the borrower's control and temporary in nature and unlikely to occur again to even be considered.

Veterans Administration (VA)

A VA loan is a mortgage backed by the Department of Veterans Affairs (VA). It is for those who have served (veterans) or who are presently serving in the U.S. military (active duty), or military spouses who qualify. The VA does not actually lend the money, they just back the money (or guarantee) 25% of a home loan up to the maximum allowable. The loans are made by the private lenders. The guarantee means the lender is protected against loss if the owner later defaults. This guarantee replaces the protection the lender normally requires with either a down payment or private mortgage insurance. So, the biggest benefit is there is no down payment.

The loans are specifically designed for military personnel, veterans, and military families. This list can include veterans, active duty personnel, reservists, national guard, and some surviving spouses. Eligibility is defined as veterans who served on active duty and have

Loan Types

a discharge, other than dishonorable, after a minimum of ninety days of service during wartime or a minimum of 181 continuous days during peacetime. There is a two-year requirement if the veteran began service after September 7, 1980 or was an officer and began service after October 16, 1981. There is a six-year requirement for National Guard and reservists, with certain criteria and specific rules concerning the eligibility of surviving spouses.

A buyer must have decent credit, income to qualify, and a valid certificate of eligibility. The home must be used as the primary home. The VA doesn't have specific credit score requirements, however, the lender will usually require a middle score somewhere between 600 and 620. This depends on each lender.

VA loans also have upfront funding fees that can be rolled into the loan. The funding fee is a percentage of the loan amount, which varies based on the type of loan and the military category, whether you are a first-time or subsequent loan user, and whether you make a down payment. You do not have to pay the fee if you are a:

- Veteran receiving VA compensation for service-connected disability OR
- Veteran who would be entitled to receive compensation for a service-connected disability if you did not receive retirement or active duty pay OR
- Surviving spouse of a Veteran who died in service or from a service-connected disability.

VA has an additional requirement for residual income, or monthly income remaining after all major debts and obligations are paid. This residual income is measured to ensure borrowers and their families will have enough money to cover basic living costs (food, transportation, child care, etc.), and this amount varies based on family size and where in the country they live.

The appraisal is conducted by a VA appraiser. There are minimum property requirements that are primarily safety issues, such as lead paint, location near a high voltage transmission easement, or certain water connection issues. The appraiser will follow the basic guidelines and will report any required repairs based on the requirements.

Borrowers must wait to apply for an VA loan for two years after a Chapter 7 bankruptcy, short sale, or foreclosure. Sometimes, if credit is re-established and was caused by extenuating circumstances, you can apply between twelve and twenty-three months. After a Chapter 13 bankruptcy, you can apply after a one-year payout period has elapsed, the borrower's payment performance has been satisfactory, and all required payments are made on time. You must wait for a one-year payout period on a Chapter 13, and three years after a foreclosure. The borrower must also re-establish a positive credit history during that period. There are occasions where the time frame can be shortened if there were extenuating circumstances. Unemployment, prolonged strikes, and medical bills not covered by insurance are potential extenuating circumstances but divorce is not considered.

Other Requirements for Government Loans (FHA, VA and RD)

For all government loans, you also need what is called a clear CAIVRS. CAIVRS (credit alert verification reporting system) is a federal government system for tracking people with federal delinquencies, or those who have defaulted or been foreclosed upon for money they owe the government. This includes a defaulted government loan, federal student loans, or small business administration loans.

If your delinquency is paid in full, or is a federally-funded approved repayment plan, you may still be eligible for a government loan. However, for example, if you had a defaulted FHA loan, you would have to wait at least three years, since the government paid the lender back on the insured loan.

Specialty Qualified Mortgages

There are also specialty loans like rehabilitation and new construction loans. These are loans available that allow you to "roll in" the costs to repair a home. Rehab loans are designed to help homeowners improve their existing home or purchase a home that can benefit from upgrades, repairs, or complete renovations. This a convenient and economical way for a buyer to finance the improvements into one single loan instead of having to apply for a second mortgage or line of equity. In addition, if the house is not currently up to standards to pass an appraisal, but this is a desirable home, these loans allow the buyer to still obtain the house through a single-close mortgage. The loan amount is based on the future completed value of the property, rather than the current value.

HomeStyle Loan (Fannie Mae)

The conventional version loan is currently called a HomeStyle Loan and can actually be used for investment or rental properties (but not flipping a house). The credit score requirement is a little higher and at least 640. Properties that are eligible include primary residences of one to four, or a one-unit second home, or investment properties for rent. These are not designed for flipping a house.

The HomeStyle Renovation Mortgage provides a convenient and flexible way for borrowers considering home improvements to make repairs and renovations with a first mortgage, rather than through a second mortgage, line of equity, or other more costly methods of financing. The limit on eligible renovation funds is 75% of the lesser of the purchase price plus renovation costs, also called the "as-completed" appraised value. Usually, any type of renovation or repair is eligible as long as it is permanently affixed to the property. Renovations should be completed within a twelve-month period, although many lenders require a six-month period.

The buyer will choose their own contractor and must have a contract with the contractor. Plans and specifications must be prepared by a registered, licensed, or certified general contractor, renovation consultant, or architect. The plans and specs should fully describe all the work and provide an indication of when various jobs or stages of completion will be scheduled, including both the start and completion dates. When submitting the plans to the lender, the contractor has to be specific on the timeline. Renovations must be completed within six months of closing and any energy improvements with one hundred days. Once all the work is completed, the lender will send the appraiser back to inspect before the contractor is paid.

Some lenders will not allow any Do-It-Yourself (DIY) work, while others will follow the conventional guidelines that allow up to 10% of the completed value, and inspections are required for all work items that cost more than $5,000.

Specialty (203k Using FHA loan)

The FHA version of a rehab loan is called a 203k. Like the conventional version, you must hire qualified contractors.

There are two versions of the 203k, standard (or regular) and limited (or streamline). The regular or standard is used for properties that need structural repairs, or for any total improvements over $35,000. Buyers can do the following on a standard rehab program:

- Room addition to a home
- Gut rehab
- Add a second floor
- Structural changes
- Major landscaping
- Repairs and remodels
- Heating and cooling systems
- Roof, plumbing, decks
- And more

The program will not cover luxury improvements, like adding a pool or tennis court, to the property. It also cannot include any improvement that does not become a permanent part of the property. For a standard 203k, you will also be required to hire a certified HUD consultant to oversee the project. The fees are determined by HUD and can be seen at: https://www.federalregister. gov/documents/2016/09/07/2016-21226/single-family-mortgage-insurance-revision-of-section-203k-consultant-fee-schedule-solicitation-of

So how much can you get? On a regular 203k, the minimum is $5,000 and the maximum is the lesser of these two amounts:

The national FHA mortgage limits- https://entp.hud.gov/idapp/html/hicostlook.cfm

Loan Types

OR

110% of the after-improved value.

With a limited or streamline loan, you can get the home for the purchase price plus up to $35,000 with no minimum repair cost, plus the cost for energy improvements. The type of work done on a streamline is much more restrictive. There can be no structural changes, room additions, or luxury improvements. Work that is permitted is:

- Kitchen and bath remodeling
- Finishing an attic or basement
- Roofing and new windows
- Repairs that are not structural
- Patios and porches
- New siding weatherization
- Updating mechanicals
- New appliances

Rural Development also has a rehab program. The regular RD loan requirements are still in place, however, this allows the buyer to repair or rehab the house with one loan. Just about any work is allowed as the long as the maximum repair amount is not exceeded. The work must be done by a general contractor. The renovation can be financed with only one monthly payment and zero percent down. There is also a streamline versus full. These are designed for single family primary use.

A streamline are repairs from $1,000 to 10,000 and using only one contractor, and must be done in thirty days.

A full is between $1,000 and $32,000 of repairs with one general contractor and up to three sub-contractors, and up fifty-nine days to complete

Health and safety issues, HVAC, roof gutter, plumbing, weatherization (windows and roofs), minor nonstructural remodeling are allowed repairs. You can add appliances if you have at $3,000 of basic repairs. Ineligible improvements include cosmetic items, decorating items, structural repairs, room additions, garages, pools/hot tubs, and landscaping.

There is a contingency reserve of $750 or 15% of repair costs, whichever is greater, and can be financed or paid in cash.

New Construction

A construction to permanent loan is a loan where you borrow money to pay for the construction costs of building the home. Once the home is complete, the loan is converted into a permanent loan. Because this is basically a two-in-one loan, meaning you close once, your closing costs are reduced, saving you money. During the construction of your home, you only pay interest on the outstanding balance, you don't have to worry about paying principal yet. Once the construction is complete, it becomes a permanent mortgage. Conventional, FHA, RD, and VA all have versions of a new construction "single-close loan."

Because construction loans are more risky than traditional loans, not all banks or financial institutions will do them. In addition to all the normal buyer documentation required, there are builder requirements. The lender needs to prove the builder is qualified for the project. The lender will require the following before proceeding:

- Adequate description of the intended materials to be used
- Resume of the builder showcasing past history of building houses
- References from the builder
- Copy of the credentials of the builder including, but not limited to, licenses, insurance, personal tax returns, and proof of adequate liability insurance
- A final copy of the building plans
- A written budget
- Contract detailing all of the construction to be done, signed by the builder and buyer
- Proof of ownership of land and whether owned by builder or buyer
- Any other lender specific required documents

Bond Loans

Low to middle income families who want to buy a home may be able to get a bond loan. Bond loans are issued by state and local authorities and subsidize the cost of becoming a homeowner for those who meet certain income and asset qualifications. Usually, they are lower interest rate programs and/or offer cash assistance. These are usually offered by state or local government agencies and each program has their own set of guidelines. Check with your lender to see if there are any available in your area.

Condos

When purchasing a condo, there are extra steps because the loan can be riskier for the lender. What makes condo loans challenging is the condo association also has to qualify in order for the mortgage to be approved. The lender has to follow guidelines from FHA, RD, VA, Fannie Mae or Freddie Mac.

For FHA, the condo must be on the FHA approved condo list: https://entp.hud.gov/idapp/html/condlook.cfm. For conventional, the lender has to verify the financial health of the association. Lenders need to see at least 85% of HOA dues paid on time, adequate and appropriate insurance for the association, adequate budget reserves, no pending litigation that could result in costly legal fees and lawsuits, and a limited number of units owned by one person or entity.

VA has their own approved list: https://vip.vba.va.gov/portal/VBAH/VBAHome/condopudsearch.

RD will usually allow a condo if it is approved by one of the other agencies. If you can finance a condo with one of the standard programs, it is considered a warrantable condo. There are lenders that will finance non-warrantable condos, however, they fall into the non-QM loans.

Non-qualified or non-QM loans

Just as the name implies, a non-qualified loan does not comply with the qualified mortgage rules and generally does not fit one of the standard conventional, FHA, RD, or VA loans. A qualified mortgage is when a lender has qualified a borrower's ability to repay their

Mortgage Loan Secrets

mortgage loan. After the housing crisis in 2008, many regulations and agencies were put into place to protect the borrower. These are not necessarily riskier loans as the buyer oftentimes will require a higher credit score, or higher income, or more assets.

These loans are often considered "out-of-the-box" loans. Usually, rates and fees are higher due to the limited liquidity the lender has to sell their loans on the secondary market. Non-QM loans cannot be sold to Fannie Mae or Freddie Mac (the conventional outlets) or guaranteed by FHA, RD, or VA.

The biggest advantage is for those who have recently had a chapter 7, 13, or foreclosure and cannot qualify for a qualified mortgage. Usually 20% down is required because the lender cannot get PMI, or private mortgage insurance, on these types of loans.

Chapter Four

Interest Rates

Now that you have chosen your loan program, what about the interest rate? That seems to be the first question everyone asks and, yet, it is not the most important question. When you see rates quoted, usually they are for a larger loan amount, 20% or more down, and a credit score of 780 or better. Most people do not fall into this category, so your lender needs to put you in the correct program with the right down payment and monthly payments.

What is the difference between my interest rate and APR?

The interest rate is the cost you will pay each year to borrow the money, expressed as a percentage rate. An annual percentage rate (APR) is a wider measure of the cost to you to borrow the money. In general, the APR not only reflects the interest rate but also any points, fees, or other charges that you pay to get the loan. For this reason, your APR is usually higher than your interest rate. It is important to remember that your APR doesn't affect your monthly payment.

What type of interest rate?

There are different options available for financing. You can get a fixed rate over different periods of time, like a thirty year or fifteen year fixed mortgage. Fifteen year mortgages are typically at a lower interest rate, however, your payment will be higher because you are paying it off in half the time. This will result in less money being paid for interest over the life of the loan. You can effectively do the same with a thirty year mortgage, by paying it off like a fifteen year loan, of course depending on the difference in interest rates. On a fixed rate loan, you pay the same payment each month, but the amount that goes to principal and interest changes monthly. The way the formula works is that, after you make your payment, it calculates what the principal balance is and computes the interest on that portion, and that is how much will be applied to interest and the balance to principal. This is why, when you pay an additional amount of money and apply it to principal, the next month more money goes toward principal.

There are also adjustable rate mortgages (ARMS). Unlike a fixed rate, where the interest rate doesn't change, an adjustable interest rate changes or adjusts based on a formula. This means your payment can go down or up. Generally, the initial interest rate is lower than a fixed interest rate. For example, you might see a 5/1 ARM. This means the introductory or initial rate is good for five years and then the interest rate can change every year after that. You can see 3/1, 7/1, or 10/1 ARMS offered.

The interest rate adjustment is based on an index. The index is an interest rate set by market conditions and published by a neutral party. To set the ARM rate, the lender takes the index rate and adds an agreed-upon number of percentage points which are called the margin. The index rate can change but the margin cannot. Most adjustable rates are tied to one of three indices: 1) One year Treasury Bill; 2) 11th District cost of funds index (COFI), the interest financial institutions pay on deposits; or 3) London Interbank Offered Rate (LIBOR), the rate most international banks are charging each other on large loans. This is being phased out in 2021. When interest rates go up, these indexes will go up. Likewise, when rates go down, these indexes will go down also. They will follow the general trend but not track exactly with current interest rates.

The margin is the percentage added to the index to determine your new interest rate, and generally runs between 2% and 4%. For example, if the index averages 4% and your margin is 3%, your rate will adjust to 7%. The index plus margin is the fully indexed rate. Margins are added for profitability to the lender because indexed rates are usually very low interest rates.

Don't worry, though, there are caps set on these types of loans. Caps can come in many flavors: 1) a periodic rate cap, which limits how much the interest rate can change from one year to the next; 2) a lifetime rate cap which limits how much the interest rate can rise over the life of the loan; or 3) a payment cap which limits the amount the monthly payment can rise over the life of the loan in dollars, versus

Interest Rates

how much the interest rate can change. One important warning is that, if the index goes up more than the cap amount in one year, the interest rate can continue to adjust the next year even if the index hasn't moved since the previous adjustment. So, for example, let's say the index has risen 1.5% in one year, but then doesn't increase for the next few years. In year one, your interest rate goes up .5% or the amount the periodic adjustment cap will allow. Then, in the next 2 years the interest rate will rise .5% consecutively until your interest rate matches the index plus margin account.

Some ARMS have a floor, an interest rate below which the rate cannot go. In other words, even if interest rates decline substantially, your new rate may not go down at all.

So, for example, if your index rate is 3 percent and your margin is 2 percent, then your fully indexed interest rate would be 5 percent.

These loans can be good for buyers who plan on selling within the next few years. However, they are riskier for the buyer because interest rates will probably go up and, hence, the payment will also. Since many people don't even keep the same mortgage for five years, a 5/1 ARM may give you plenty of time to sell or refinance your home without your rate ever adjusting. Another advantage is it might help you qualify for a bigger home. Because the initial payment is often lower it can be easier to qualify for a larger loan. Often, first- ime home buyers will use this if they expect to earn more money in five years than they do now.

Some of the disadvantages include lack of consistency in payments, especially if your rate adjusts frequently. In this type of program, your initial interest rate is often artificially low so your payment could very well go up when the interest rates reset, especially if you were planning on selling or refinancing before the first adjustment and that didn't happen.

What is a buydown?

A buydown is a financing technique where the buyer gets a lower interest rate for at least the first few years. Buydowns are like a subsidy from the seller to the buyer. Typically, the seller contributes

Mortgage Loan Secrets

funds to an escrow account that subsidizes the loan during the first few years, resulting in initial lower payments. Buydowns usually last a few years and then the payment increases to the standard rate once it expires.

For example, in a 3-2-1 buydown, the buyer pays a lower payment for the first three years. These payments are offset by the contribution from the seller. Let's say the homeowner gets a 6.75% fixed interest rate. In year one they would pay 3.75%, in year two 4.75%, and in year three 5.75%. In the years following the first three years, their payment would increase to the standard 6.75% rate. While they received a savings from the lower interest rate, the difference in the payments would have been made by the seller to the lender as a subsidy.

A 2-1 buydown is very similar, however the discount is only for the first two years. In the same example of a 6.75% rate the first year the buyer would pay 4.75% and in year two 5.75% then the following years are back at the 6.75% rate.

Chapter Five

Where do you get a loan?

So now you have your documents, you chose a loan program with your loan officer, and decided on the best type of interest rate for you. Let's talk about where your loan officer works and the type of institution it is.

Loan officers work with buyers and counsels them on choosing the best mortgage program and assists with the loan application. Loan officers can work for a depository bank, a mortgage bank, or a broker. Loan officers can have various names sometimes: mortgage consultants, loan originators, loan consultants, and mortgage planners. Starting August 1, 2009, any individual who, for compensation or gain, takes a residential mortgage loan application, or offers or negotiates terms of a residential mortgage loan application, must be licensed or registered as a Mortgage Loan Originator.

Lending institutions can be a depository bank like community banks, credit unions, and savings and loan companies. Typically, they have many functions in addition to mortgage lending like checking and saving accounts, personal loans, car, and other types of loans. Many times, these companies loan money from their deposit accounts and then they can keep the loans internally.

Other lending institutions are mortgage bankers. Their only job is usually issuing mortgage loans. Typically, they sell their loans in the secondary market to investors such as Fannie Mae and Freddie Mac.

Both of these are direct lenders. They close and fund a mortgage with their own funds. Usually, the processing, underwriting, and appraisal services are handled within the company, giving the loan officer a little more control.

A broker is an intermediary loan officer. They will look at your loan application and match you with a lender, but they do not use their own funds to originate mortgages. They also do not have any control over the internal process as it is in the hands of the actual lender.

Chapter Six

The Actual Mortgage

So, after you have collected all of the necessary documents, what happens next? Your loan officer will review the documents and, based on the information you provided, will issue a preapproval and your home search begins. Once you have found a house and made an offer that was accepted, the actual loan process begins. You will be given the application, with all the information you provided, in either an electronic form or printed to sign. At this time, you will decide if you want to lock in your rate, or if you want to wait until further along in the mortgage process. You and your loan officer should discuss the plusses and minuses of locking versus waiting. There will be many sheets of paper and disclosures that you will have to sign based on government regulations. One of the most important ones is called your loan estimate. A sample can be found at: https://www.consumerfinance.gov/ask-cfpb/what-is-a-loan-estimate-en-1995/.

Essentially, the loan estimate is a three-page document telling you the important details about the loan you requested, and it must be provided within three business days of your application. This form provides you with the interest rate, monthly payment, and total closing costs for the loan. It will also give you information about your estimated costs for taxes and insurance, and how the interest rate and payments can change in the future if you are not on a fixed-term loan. It will also indicate any special features like a prepayment penalty or a negative amortization feature. The form uses clear language and all lenders are required to use the same form.

What is the difference between my principal and interest payment and my total payment (PITI)?

The principal and interest payment is the main component of your mortgage payment. The principal is the amount of money you are borrowing and the interest is what you are charged by the lender for borrowing the money. Unless you have a variable rate loan this cannot change throughout the life of the loan. For most people, the amount of money you send monthly to your lender will include other things, like property taxes, home owners insurance, any monthly mortgage insurance, and flood insurance if required. This money is held in an escrow or impound account until the amounts are due and then the lender will pay those bills. Most loans require an escrow or impound account to be set up because the lender will pay those bills when due, and the lender is then assured that the bills are paid. If you live in a condo, or anything with a homeowners association, those fees will show up in your total payment due, even if you pay them yourself.

Usually, once a year the servicer of your loan will send you an escrow analysis showing how much money came into your escrow or impound account and what bills were paid. If you have a shortage, because taxes or insurance went up, you will have to pay the difference. Depending on the amount, you may have a choice as to whether to include the amounts in your future payments, or you may be required to submit the complete shortage at that time. So, an increase in insurance or taxes could very well make a payment go up in the future.

The Loan heads to the Processor

After all the documents are signed and submitted, the loan will continue through the process. Although all lenders do things slightly differently, most will send your file to a processor. At this time, the processor will review all the documents you provided and make sure all the documents are current and that nothing is missing. They do not evaluate the numbers or analyze any documents. They simply do a "double check" that all the required documents are submitted. Often, the processor will order your title work, a verification of employment, and perhaps a copy of your tax transcripts, or any other paperwork required.

Once all the documents are submitted and reviewed, the file passes over to an underwriter.

The "Dreaded" Underwriter

The underwriter is a person the buyer will never meet and, yet, they are the most important person in the process. No lender will fund or

The Actual Mortgage

close a loan without an underwriter's approval. The underwriter is a person hired by the loan company to make sure that the loan fits into the parameters of the lending guidelines. They double-check all the loan officer's numbers for income, assets, and liabilities, etc. They must verify the income and stable job history, debt ratios, credit history, and verify that the debt falls within all acceptable limits. The guidelines for each loan are hundreds of pages long and the underwriter, like the loan officer, needs to be familiar with those guidelines. The underwriter will also verify that all tax, title, insurance, and closing documentation is in place. The underwriter may, and often will, ask for additional documentation to verify items or things they may not understand.

What is a manual and automated underwrite?

Most loans are "run through" an automated underwriter program, or AUS, by the loan officer before ever turning in a file. The numbers that are used are keyed in by a loan officer or assistant and the system uses those figures in their formulas. Each loan program has its own system and set of rules. Once the loan officer has entered everything and "runs" the program, it will come back with either an eligible, refer, or deny result. If it is an eligible or accept, the loan officer can move it forward through the normal process. Even in those cases, the underwriter will still do their due diligence and verify everything submitted. If the physical documents do not match the AUS, the underwriter will send the file back with conditions. This gives the loan officer another opportunity to clarify or update any incorrect documents. Once those documents are corrected, the file will go back to the underwriter for further review.

Many times, a loan file requires what is called a "manual" underwrite because it falls into a gray area that an automated system cannot address. Manually underwritten files for FHA, RD, and VA can be common, since they are more flexible with credit and debt issues. The loan officer will have additional work and has to carefully compile manual files to read more like a story, with lots of supporting detail. Those files will not only provide the basic information, but may also include a created credit history for people who have no credit score, additional information about any credit hiccups in the past, or explanations for discrepancies in income or job history information. This documentation gives the underwriter "the whys" and allows them to make a more informed decision about how solid the risk would be.

An underwriter is taking a calculated risk in a manual underwriting and will take extra precautions in, not just the letter of the guidelines, but the intent. It is a judgement call and is based on how much risk the company is willing to take. If they are wrong, and the loan defaults, it is not only expensive to the lender, it can cost the company the ability to fund those types of loans.

Appraisal

Meanwhile, simultaneously, the appraisal is ordered. The appraiser is hired by the lender; however, the appraiser is an independent, licensed person who verifies that the amount the buyer is paying matches what the property is worth. In addition, depending on the type of loan, they have to make sure the house is safe from obvious defects. An appraisal is not a home inspection and a home inspection is not an appraisal.

A home inspection is an objective visual examination of the physical structure and systems of a house. Home inspectors are usually employed by the prospective home buyer and done before the loan is even submitted. A home inspector hired by a buyer works in the best interest of the client, the home buyer. An appraiser looks at the house from a financial perspective. They appraise the value of the house based on square footage, lot size, and many other factors. They also look at property values of other houses in the neighborhood to get a better understanding. In addition, they need to check for major defects such as holes in the roof, safety issues, and anything that would lower the value of the property. Once the appraiser submits a report, the underwriter or appraisal department will review the document and verify that the comparable houses that were used were reasonable based on size and location. The underwriter can ask for modifications or clarifications to statements made. The appraisal will also state that the appraisal is either "as is" or "subject to". If it is "as is," in the appraiser's opinion nothing needs to be done to the property to give it the value it has been assigned. If it is "subject to," the appraiser is stating that certain items must be completed before the loan can close. This becomes the responsibility of the seller to have these items completed. Once they are done, the appraiser will go back out and verify and update the report. There are occasions when a repair cannot be done before close due to weather issues. When this happens an escrow account will need to be set up to handle the payment after the close. Not all lenders allow escrow repairs.

A home inspector looks at the house from a structural perspective. They look at the electrical, plumbing, age of the roof, and the HVAC systems, and make sure everything is safe. They make sure everything is working and properly connected. They look to see if there is any structural damage, water damage, mold, and any other potential problems. It is highly recommended that you always get a home inspection before buying any property.

What is title insurance?

Along with an appraisal being ordered, title work is also ordered. There are two sides to the title work, the one ordered by the lender to protect the lender, and the one to protect the buyer. They both serve two different purposes.

The lender's title insurance protects the lender against problems with the title to your property, such as a someone with a legal claim against the home. Lender's title only protects the lender against problems with the title. It is paid for by the buyer as part of their closing costs.

An owner's policy provides protection to the homeowner if someone sues and says they have a claim against the home from before the homeowner purchased it. Common claims come from a previous owner's failure to pay taxes, or from contractors who say they were not paid for work done on the house. In many states, the buyer will ask the seller to pay for this title insurance when they write the offer. When this happens, often the seller will choose the title company and not the buyer, as the seller is paying.

After the final reviews are done

Once the appraisal and title comes back and the underwriter has reviewed all your documents, your file starts the closing process. There are often two steps before the final documents are drawn and you are signing at the closing table. The first is that the underwriter issues you a "final approval." This means the underwriter does not need to see any more documents. However, it may not mean you are done yet. Now, the file will go back to a processor. They will make sure you haven't taken on any new debt and they will verify employment again, order your homeowners insurance, make sure any required documents that were ordered from an outside party are all in, like tax transcripts, requested changes to title work, or appraisals. Even loan officers can confuse the difference between final approval and the final "clear to close" words. If there is a delay in receiving any of this information, or it comes back and does not match up with what was provided by the borrower, it can cause a delay in closing. It is often, at this time, that you will receive what is called an initial closing disclosure.

An initial closing disclosure is a document that must by law be provided to you at least three days before your closing. It is a key document that gives you more details about your loan, key terms, and how much you are paying in fees and other costs to get your mortgage. Most of the numbers should be exactly the same as the loan estimate you signed, except for items you were allowed to "shop for" and, even those, shouldn't be more than 10% from the loan estimate. If something had changed dramatically in the loan process, like changing a loan program and deciding to switch to a fifteen year versus a thirty year loan, you would have received an updated loan estimate at the time of the change. You will often be required to sign that you received this document so the three-day waiting period can begin.

There are some items that might change based on the actual date of closing like proration, updated property tax or insurance, or interest charged from the day you close to the end of the month. The purpose, product, sales price, loan amount, loan term, and interest rate should not have changed from the estimate provided on the Loan Estimate.

A sample can be found at:

https://files.consumerfinance.gov/f/201403_cfpb_closing-disclosure_cover-H25B.pdf

The Closing

All the required documents are in, you have received your initial closing disclosure for review, and you are ready to close. The lender's closer works with the title or escrow company to work up your final numbers and documents.

The "closing" is the last step in buying and financing a home. It is also called the settlement and it is when you and all the other parties in the transaction sign the necessary documents. Once you sign those documents, you are legally responsible for the mortgage loan and the legal owner of your new home. Depending on the state, all parties may sit around a table and sign the documents at the same time, or the closing could take longer when the signatures of each party are collected separately. Some of the people that might attend your closing:

- Your realtor or real estate agent
- Your title insurance company
- An escrow company
- Your attorney (some states require attorneys to conduct closings) or if you hire legal representation
- The seller's attorney
- Your lender

Some of the many documents you may sign at closing include:

- A promissory note which describes details regarding your loan
- A mortgage or security instrument that explains your responsibilities and rights as a borrower, and which grants the lender or servicer the right to foreclose on your home if you fail to make payments as agreed.
- Any state and local government mandated documents
- Lender documents

Usually you will owe money at closing. Some title or escrow companies will require those funds in a wire transfer or a certified or cashier's check. Normally, you cannot pay any fees with a personal check or cash. After all documents are signed and verified by the title/escrow/attorney and the lender, the funds are disbursed, the seller transfers ownership to you, and it is recorded at your local government agency.

In addition to having a house warming party, you will need to secure your documents. You may receive a paper copy or a digital copy of your mortgage. Just be sure to keep it in a secure location. You will also want to change your driver's license, file homestead taxes with your government and agency, switch utilities into your name, and update anyone who needs your new address.

Making your payments

Typically, your first house payment is not due until the first of the following month in which you closed. So, if you close anytime in May, your first payment will not be due until July.

A common question is, "Will my loan be sold?" There are two aspects to this—one is the interest in the loan, and one is the servicing of the loan. Most do not understand the difference. Most lenders always sell the interest in the loan. In this case, if a lender is a direct lender, they will sell the interest in the mortgage to an agency like Fannie Mae, Freddie Mac, or Ginnie Mae. This enables the lender to raise ready cash, improving liquidity and allowing them to make more loans.

Fannie Mae (Federal National Mortgage Association) is a government-sponsored enterprise, or GSE, with the mission of bringing liquidity, stability, and affordability to the U.S. housing market. It does this by purchasing mortgages from lenders, and then selling them, through a process calling securitization. Securitizing is the process of pooling mortgages and selling them to investors. Usually, the bank retains the servicing rights, and most borrowers never know their loans are owned by one of the agencies.

The Actual Mortgage

Servicing

Even though the interest in the loan has been sold, often the lender will retain servicing rights. However, they do have the right at any time to sell the servicing rights also. This is very common and it cannot affect the loan rate, terms, or amount owed. The bottom line is that you will simply need to make your monthly payment to a different company.

The servicer collects and processes the borrower's payment. It will manage communications with the borrower. It will pay the taxes and insurance from escrows. If the loan is sold or transferred, and the servicer changes, here is what to expect.

You will receive two notices. One will come from your current servicer, internally called a "goodbye letter." The other notice will come from your new servicer, called a "welcome letter." Under no circumstances should you start sending your payment to someone who is sending you a welcome letter without receiving a good bye letter. Fraud is prevalent, and your mortgage is public record, and unscrupulous people will convince you to send them the payment instead of your current servicer. Whenever in doubt, contact your loan officer.

Usually a borrower's current servicer must notify you no less than fifteen days before the effective date of the transfer. Review the notice carefully. It must contain the following:

- Name and address of the new servicer
- When the current servicer will stop accepting your payments
- The date the new servicer will begin accepting your payments
- The date the first mortgage payment is due to the new servicer
- Telephone numbers for the current and new servicer
- Whether you can continue optional insurance like credit, life, or disability
- A statement that the transfer will not affect any terms or conditions of your mortgage, except those directly related to the servicing of the loan; for example, if you currently are

Mortgage Loan Secrets

not required to have an escrow account, your new servicer cannot demand you establish one

- A statement explaining your rights and what to do if you have a question or complaint about your loan servicing

Other do's and don'ts:

- If you have your payment automatically withdrawn from your account, confirm that those payments will continue and, if not, ask for the proper paperwork to sign up with the new servicer.
- If you send payments directly and automatically from your bank account (instead of the lender withdrawing them), update the payment information and pay close attention to the effective date of transfer.
- If you mail payments, verify the new address and the new account number for the loan with the new servicer.
- A week or two after the first payment with your new servicer, contact them and verify they received your payment; there is a grace period for misdirected payments, so use this time to ensure your payments are working smoothly.
- Never send payment to a new servicer/address until you have received a transfer/sale notice.
- Whenever in doubt, contact your current servicer or loan officer.
- Don't fight the transfer or sale. You cannot prevent it.

Conclusion

Overall, when obtaining a mortgage, you not only want to be prepared with paperwork and information, you want the right loan officer. You want a loan officer who understands the process, and who is familiar with the programs and can ask all the right questions so you are in the right program. A dedicated and true loan officer will act as your financial advisor on the debt side.

Your loan officer should do all of the following:

- Discuss your current situation and objectives for the current mortgage.
- Evaluate and compare loan options so you understand how they affect you long-term.
- Provide you with the most positive experience through communication, education, and competence.
- Continue to maintain a life-time relationship and do annual reviews.

Overall, while you are in the process of purchasing your home, you want to make it the most boring time of your life, financially that is.

This is the usually the largest purchase of your life. Choose the right officer.

Did you enjoy this informative guide?

...then it would be wonderful if you could leave a review on Amazon and share your thoughts.

This would also help other potential readers to decide whether this book could be helpful to them.

Your help is much appreciated and you can post your review here.

Printed in Poland
by Amazon Fulfillment
Poland Sp. z o.o., Wrocław